Also by Carl Phillips

Poetry

In the Blood
Cortège
From the Devotions
Pastoral
The Tether
Rock Harbor
The Rest of Love
Riding Westward
Quiver of Arrows: Selected Poems, 1986–2006
Speak Low
Double Shadow
Silverchest
Reconnaissance
Wild Is the Wind

Prose

Coin of the Realm: Essays on the Life and Art of Poetry

The Art of Daring: Risk, Restlessness, Imagination

As Editor

Firsts: 100 Years of Yale Younger Poets

Translation

Philoctetes

STAR
MAP
WITH ACTION
FIGURES

Star Map with Action Figures
Copyright © 2019 by Carl Phillips

Cover art: Freepik.com

Author photograph courtesy of the author

Cover design by Seth Pennington

Sibling Rivalry Press, LLC
PO Box 26147
Little Rock, AR 72221

info@siblingrivalrypress.com

www.siblingrivalrypress.com

ISBN: 978-1-943977-65-9

By special invitation, this title is housed in the Rare Book and Special Collections Vault of the Library of Congress.

First Sibling Rivalry Press Edition, September 2019

STAR
MAP
WITH ACTION
FIGURES

CARL PHILLIPS

SIBLING RIVALRY PRESS
DISTURB/ENRAPTURE
LITTLE ROCK, ARKANSAS

Once someone enters your mind, no matter where he is you can dream about him—someone can dream about *you*, whether you've given permission or not... If someone dreams about you, does it keep you alive?

Deborah Eisenberg

CONTENTS

AND IF I FALL

There's this cathedral in my head I keep
making from cricket song and
dying but rogue-in-spirit, still,
bamboo. Not making. I keep
imagining it, as if that were the same
thing as making, and as if making might
bring it back, somehow, the real
cathedral. In anger, as in desire, it was
everything, that cathedral. As if my body
itself cathedral. I conduct my body
with a cathedral's steadiness, I
try to. I cathedral. In desire. In anger.
Light enters a cathedral the way persuasion fills a body.
Light enters a cathedral, the way persuasion fills a body.

DANGEROUS ONLY WHEN DISTURBED

Of birdsongs, I know only three
for certain: cardinal, blue jay, raven,
though perhaps the last two
don't count—not as song. More call
than song. More cry, by which I mean
exclamatory, not the kind
with tears. Not that tears
can't be song sometimes, depending on
who's weeping, for what reason, and
with what degree of restraint, finally, at least
half of what any music worth being
called music's made of; as for the rest—
release? Does that still
sound right? Did you know the blue
of the blue morpho butterfly's
iridescent wings isn't biological
but an engineering of light, that they're
not blue at all? In the song
of you, in the song I make of you,
in which your horselessness means
a fear of horses, nothing
more than that, you're a man asleep
beneath the willow's umbrella, you've
grown your hair out, the hair rises
the way dream does to the cool
descent of the willow's branches, from
the thicket that hair and branches and
dream make, I haven't
forgotten you, it's just I've been
distracted, between the sound
of birds singing somewhere and this

inability to keep any song left
inside me from ruining
everything, or so I tell myself, and
like that, if not true as in
provable, as in *here's proof*, it's true enough
to believe in. You're awake, I think.
Your mouth is moving.

WAKE UP

The road down from everything even you had hardly dared
to hope for has its lonely stretches, yes, but it's hard to feel alone
entirely: there's a river that runs beside it the whole way down,
and there's an over-song that keeps the river company: I'm leaves,
you're the wind…

         I used to think the song had to do with the leaves'
confusion, the wind letting up, their mistaking this for something
like courtesy on the wind's part, or even forgiveness. But leaves don't
get confused. Silly, to think it. And what can leaves know of courtesy,
let alone forgiveness? What's forgiveness?

             Wake up, for the falconer
has lost his falcon. He has heard that falcons are like memory, they
come back. But not all memories do, not all memories should. If
anyone knows this, it's the falconer. How long ago that was… Yet

all the varieties of good fortune he's come upon, as a hand comes
idly upon an orchard's windfalls, how different he's become since—
none of it matters, when the falconer steps back into memory as into
a vast cathedral, which is to say, when he remembers.

            How cool it is,
inside the cathedral. And at first, how dark. Soon, though, he can see
a chapel set aside for prayers specifically to the virgin whose story he's
always resisted. He sees a corner where people have lit candles, sometimes
for another's suffering, sometimes for their own. He sees the altar with
the falcon sitting on top of it.

The weight of grief over what's lost,
versus the shadow of what's lost—forever struggling to return, and failing:
who can say which is better? The falconer's eye meets the falcon's eye:

I have a story, the falcon says, seems to, the wings lifting, the feathers
rippling with a story's parts—I have a story; I can't wait to tell you.

ON TRIUMPH

If done steadily, and with the kind of patience that belies all fear,
it is indeed possible to walk the plank backwards from the doom
of vanishing

to that softer, wildflowered field across which mere
diminishment winds like a path maybe worth sticking to, finally, for look
where the alternatives have led—not that, even now, you regret them,
or would, if you believed in regret,

if you could understand regret
in all of its steepness, the slim shadow it has a way of casting—like
a finger at the lips, for silence—across that chaos whose names,
so it seems, change endlessly: unreason, consciousness, the sea with its
shifting patterns, now fluorescence and glitter, now glitter and shine,
mirrors

wasted on the usual mob that, forever strange to it, spits
on triumph as if triumph were tangible, meant both to protect the chest
and give a certain grace to it, like chainmail, but not made of metal
this time—instead, glass bells:

so small;
each gently hitting the next, beside it;
plovers piping from the low sea-grass that barely hides them;

UNBRIDLED

To look at them, you might not think the two men, having spoken briefly
   and now moving away from each other, as different goals
  require, have much history, if any,
between them. That for a time that seems longer ago now than in fact
   it's been, they used to enter each other's bodies so often, so routinely,
  yet without routine ever seeming the right way of putting it,
that even they lost count—for back then,
    who counted? It's not as if they've forgotten, or at least
  the one hasn't, looking long enough back at the other
to admire how outwardly unchanged he seems: still muscled, even if
   each muscle most brings to mind (why, though)
  an oracle done hiding at last, all the mystery made
quantifiable, that it might more easily that way—like love, like the impulse
   toward love—be disassembled. The other man doesn't look back
  at all, or think to, more immediately distracted
by the dog he had half-forgotten at the end of a leash he'd forgotten
   entirely, though here it is, in his hand,
  and the dog at the end of it. What kind of dog? The kind whose
digging beneath the low-lying branches of a bush thick with flowers
   shakes the flowers loose, they make of the dog's
  furious back a fury of petals that the dog takes no notice of,
though the man has noticed.
   How the petals lie pattern-less where they've fallen.
  How there's a breeze, bit of storm in it. How as if in response
the dog lifts its dirt-blackened face from the hole it's digging,
   then continues digging. Then the man is crying. No it *looks* like crying.
  Now what good at this point do you really think that's likely to do
either of us, he says, to the dog.

WE TURN HERE

If we don't have to bring honesty into this,
      why bring it, or that's at least what I
            think the question was, though what I more
remember is how it kept breaking—
      the question did—the way waves do,
            touching shore (one, that I shall be punished,
two, that this is not yet the punishment) each wave eventually
      indistinguishable from the wave before.

TO LIE DOWN. TO WEAR NOTHING AT ALL.

And then just like that, with hardly anyone
noticing, it became daily harder to remember when
this sense of being at sea had begun—at sea, as in
on a wave of doubt mixed with fear and yet no small
amount, incongruously, of fevered anticipation, not joy
itself but the belief, still—the half-belief—some joy
might come. Maybe
                    the beginning doesn't matter anyway—
whatever wasn't the case once, it's the case now, long
days of jazz and drinks named after jazz, Give me a John
Coltrane, someone saying; another, I'll take one more
round of these Take Fives…Not that there aren't
those who suspect the headiness of this new weather
will soon enough dissipate, the holler-and-buzz
surrounding it will follow suit. We're alike in that way,
you and I—comrades, if you will, in our shared
suspicion, whether you know it yet or not, says
the captain to the young man across the room,
who of course can't hear him because the captain has
only said this to himself, not aloud yet. He looks at
the young man,
                    who hasn't yet seen the captain. It's as if
he's trying not to look. Look at me, thinks the captain. And
the young man's head starts to turn toward him. Any
moment he'll see the captain for the first time. The way
all histories begin, apparently. What destroys finding
what will be destroyed, though which is which has yet to be
determined. Almost lavender, the captain's eyes are, in this light.

REASONABLE DOUBT

What it looked like?

Like fucking the forest for once birdless, beastless.

Like measuring the distance between all that's lost
and everything else that, even now, waved at
hard enough sometimes,
will sometimes wave back.

But it felt like swallowing the sea—
being forced to, ships and all.

Then a silence as vast as it was particular.

Then like holding a mirror up to Apollo
and expecting his face there, when Apollo's always been
faceless, obviously, being a god.

And the hand still holding the mirror up anyway.

And the face not showing.

FINE

I have a story. In this story, there's a set of doors,
shut, medieval—
at least they look medieval—across the blue
tops of which someone has spray-painted—
but carefully, in gold, like an updated,
somehow sluttier, therefore
sturdier version of gold leaf—two sentences:
        Tell me what enters.
        Speak of what's forever getting left behind.
Sentences that, ever since their
overnight-three-weeks-ago appearance,
no one calls sentences, everyone here
calls them prayers. How does a sentence,

just like that, become prayer? What's prayer anyway? From
a window not far but, from here, not visible, I think now
it's better, maybe, that we not speak again
ever, someone has just said to no one answering. I can't
hear an answer. It's the kind of
town, still, where no one locks the doors,

you can step inside.
Step inside.
Imagine the dreamer's difficulty—
try to: the sheer weight, of course, of dream;
the not-yet-broken-to-ride horse;
the hanged man's naked body, athletic
even now, especially now, stopped
in stillness, "Wilderness has been
no mystery" tattooed
across the dead man's chest Feel regret
fine—but do you have to keep speaking of it as if regret
were a game of horseshoes, or a power saw, or the sea?

AND SWEPT ALL VISIBLE SIGNS AWAY

Easy enough, to say it's dark now.
But what is the willow doing in the darkness?
I say it wants less for company than for compassion,

which can come from afar and faceless. What's a face, to a willow?
If a willow had a face, it would be a song, I think.
I am stirred, I'm stir-able, I'm a wind-stirred thing,

the song would go...But there
is no song. As there is no face. There's just the willow
as willow. Nothing but itself. Its shadow meaningless

except to those who want for shade,
and find it there. Who keep finding they hardly
care anymore—almost, some days, as if they'd never cared—

about connection. Green as water, the willow's motion. Green as oblivion,
the willow's indifference—flecked with a little gold, some blue.

HONEST IN WHICH NOT GENTLY

Does it matter how festive it was, the setting out for far country,
the horses, their chestnut flanks, their eyes the color of black basil,
which is purple, really? Now just skulls where a face used to be,
shameless, as in bereft of shame finally, each catching the snow
gently but differently, the snow, and the wind scattering it, as if

unapparent meant nonexistent. They say language has its own sorrow,
but no word for it: does this crying out maybe come close, though,
can we say it does, to have stared into the dark and said aloud, even
if quietly, Who's there? Anyone around? Panicking too late, as is
the way with panic, the killer stumbles through woods and a snowfall

that feels like ritual and a release from ritual, so that it also feels—
at first, anyway—like being lost, but free. Beneath the pines, the two
horses stood exactly where he'd left them untethered hours ago. Snow
dusted their fine bodies. Nightmare. Nightmare Lifting. Their names
swim up to him. I remember, now. Yes. Now it's all coming back.

SELF

You plan on riding with me,
you'll have to hold on tight, I told him, or
maybe he told me, whoever I must have been or thought I was in those

days that—who remembers, now, except for there being just the two
dreams left by then,
and how hard to decide: the dream of bondage,

or the other one, not of the slow release from bondage but from
any thought or desire to go, even briefly, free, for was not freedom
a kind of bondage, too? Sometimes,

they thought that. The way that, even though they understood the self
as a thing impossible to see past,
they could still think it was worth trying to, as if the self were a vast

thicket through which, sure, the light made its way occasionally but was
mostly thwarted,
or as if the self were the horizon sea and sky make

at sunset, just before sunset, and not in fact a needle pushed through
the stretched canvas of belief then pulled back
up again, up through belief, into recognition: there are choices,

you can choose. If the bruised face in the mirror isn't what you meant to see,
or you just don't right now feel like looking at it, look away.
So you look away

24

SOUNDTRACK FOR A FRAME OF WINTER

There's a forest that stands at the exact center of sorrow.
Regrets find no shelter there.
The trees, when they sway,
sway like the manes of horses when a storm's not far.
There's no reason to stay there,
nothing worth going to see,
but if you want to you can pass through the forest
in the better part of a long day.
Who would want to, though?

To have entered the forest changes nothing about sorrow.
It's a forest. Not oblivion. Not erasure.
Some have entered it in the name of distraction,
if only briefly, from the sorrow within which
the forest thrives to no apparent purpose—fools, dreamers,
the desperate from whom it's best, if at all possible,
to look calmly away, the trees of the forest at the center of sorrow—
the exact center—all but say,
or that's what it sounds like on windier nights,

tonight, for example. At the forest's exact center,
almost impossible to find, but I have been there myself,
there's a makeshift grave, more than likely overgrown by now
with weeds, moss, the usual.
With defeat, desire, the usual.
Wingless ambition, frangible hope, misunderstanding, i.e., mistake,
another form of weakness, i.e., the usual.
That the forest itself contains no apology
doesn't mean you're not hurt. Or I'm not sorry. Or I didn't hurt you.

STAR MAP WITH ACTION FIGURES

More dark than gray, but not yet quite the truer dark
called darkness, the stories keep ending as if there were
a limit to what any story could hold onto, and this
the limit, the latest version of it, looking a lot like the sea
meeting shore.

                        *

             To constellate, the way desire
does, sometimes, with fear, or anger—both, occasionally—
and there's been gentleness, too, I'm here, I've
always been here…

                    *

             Maybe between mystery
and what little we can say for sure
happened, lies a secret even
memory itself keeps somewhere
hidden because for now
it has to.

                    *

             Less like wishing too late, I mean,
for a thing to be otherwise than like fire closing in
so absolutely, it can almost seem intimacy
had yet to be invented, and here's the fire,
inventing it: Constellate,
with me—

                    *

             Look at the field,
studded with the blue-black eyes of broken heroes.
One of the eyes is moving. It can still see. What does it see?

MY MONSTER

This hill, even if a small one, this hill with us and the dog the same dog
forever moving shadowlike down it, to where the hill disappears... For
some of a winter long ago, back when empathy still seemed a form
of love—more static, maybe, less steep, but just as complicated—
I stayed in a small house, cabin-like, but no cabin, at the end of a pier
that jutted out into a harbor the way piers do. It was January. Why so

this quiet, he used to ask, in his language. I barely knew his language.
I'd turn him over, and there was sex or not, then, and there was
sleeping after. At night as I lay in bed, the whole place would rock,
mostly gently, which was the tide finding higher shore again, or
sometimes the wind making rough with water, as was the case one
particular night when it was snowing. Snowing over the sea,

and windy. I know resemblance is not equation. I know
equivalence doesn't mean translation. I say there was a wind,
and that's often how I remember it, but tonight it almost seems
the night must have been windless, I remember the steady verticality
with which the snow fell, falling into the sea. I'd turn him over; I barely
knew him; why so this quiet. The crown looks good on you, the veil
does too—when you lift the veil, the future's everything you wished for.

ALL THE LOVE YOU'VE GOT

And now, having dismissed everyone as he
wishes he could dismiss his own dreams that make each
night restless—that same unswayable knowledge, and
the belief in it, that he is
                              king here, which means
being a stranger, at least outwardly, to even the least
trace of doubt—after all of this, the king has stepped
from the royal tent, is walking toward the sound
of water, where the river must be. There's the river,
rivering south,
                    as rivers tend to. Beside the river,
two men are fucking. Young men. Almost too young
to even know about fucking, thinks the king, who can't
help noticing how the men bring a somehow grace
to the business between them—a grace that some might
confuse with love. But the king
                                    rarely makes mistakes,
which is to say, he knows mercy when he sees it. What
does mercy have to do with fucking? What does love
have to do with grace? What are dreams but the only
rivers memory knows how to make? There's a kind of
music
        to how the men routinely but unpredictably trade
places entering and withdrawing from each other. It's as if
they're singing a song that might go, "I'm the king, no you're
the king and I'm the river, no you're the river." On and on,
like that. Leave them; they do
                                    no harm. The king making
his slow, insomnia-ed way back. The night dark but not dark
entirely: moonless, yes, but through the pines enough stars
still visible. Whoever goes there,

let me pass. Beneath
the brocaded cloak, each bead stitched to it by hand,
beneath the cloak of some more breathable, lighter fabric
beneath that, the king's cock rests like tenderness itself
against the king's left thigh. How soft the stars look.

ACKNOWLEDGMENTS

Grateful thanks to the editors of the journals where these poems first appeared:

Academy of American Poets/Poets.org: "All the Love You've Got"
American Poetry Review: "Wake Up," "We Turn Here," "And Swept
    All Visible Signs Away," "Self," "Soundtrack for a Frame of Winter"
Harvard Advocate: "Honest in Which Not Gently," "To Lie Down. To
    Wear Nothing at All"
The Journal: "Reasonable Doubt"
On the Seawall: "Fine"
Paris Review: "On Triumph," "Unbridled"
Virginia Quarterly Review: "And If I Fall," "Dangerous Only When
    Disturbed," "Star Map with Action Figures," "My Monster"

*

"And If I Fall": the title is also the title of a song by The Charlatans.

"My Monster": the title is also the title of a short story by Bo Huston.

"Star Map with Action Figures" also appeared in *The Best American Poetry 2019*, Major Jackson and David Lehman (eds.), Scribner, NY, 2019.

"And If I Fall," "Dangerous Only When Disturbed," "My Monster," and "Star Map with Action Figures" received the Emily Clark Balch Prize for Poetry from *Virginia Quarterly Review*.

ABOUT THE POET

Carl Phillips teaches at Washington University in St. Louis.

ABOUT THE PRESS

Sibling Rivalry Press is an independent press based in Little Rock, Arkansas. It is a sponsored project of Fractured Atlas, a nonprofit arts service organization. Contributions to support the operations of Sibling Rivalry Press are tax-deductible to the extent permitted by law, and your donations will directly assist in the publication of work that disturbs and enraptures. To contribute to the publication of more books like this one, please visit our website and click *donate*.

Sibling Rivalry Press gratefully acknowledges the following donors, without whom this book would not be possible:

Tony Taylor

Mollie Lacy

Karline Tierney

Maureen Seaton

Travis Lau

Michael Broder & Indolent Books

Robert Petersen

Jennifer Armour

Alana Smoot

Paul Romero

Julie R. Enszer

Clayton Blackstock

Tess Wilmans-Higgins & Jeff Higgins

Sarah Browning

Tina Bradley

Kai Coggin

Queer Arts Arkansas

Jim Cory

Craig Cotter

Hugh Tipping

Mark Ward

Russell Bunge

Joe Pan & Brooklyn Arts Press

Carl Lavigne

Karen Hayes

J. Andrew Goodman

Diane Greene

W. Stephen Breedlove

Ed Madden

Rob Jacques

Erik Schuckers

Sugar le Fae

John Bateman

Elizabeth Ahl

Risa Denenberg

Ron Mohring & Seven Kitchens Press

Guy Choate & Argenta Reading Series

Guy Traiber

Don Cellini

John Bateman

Gustavo Hernandez

Anonymous (12)

CPSIA information can be obtained
at www.ICGtesting.com
Printed in the USA
BVHW032348200120
569971BV00009B/1227